Made in United States
North Haven, CT
08 November 2022

26433486R00061